small world

Celebrating

Gwenyth Swain

ZERO TO TEN

For my grandfather Alfred P. Coman,
who knew how to celebrate the small things in life

To find out more about the pictures in this book, turn to page 22.
To find out more about sharing this book with children, turn to page 24.

The photographs in this book are reproduced through the courtesy of: © Trip/J. Sweeney, front cover; © Trip/G. Pritchard, back cover; Ling Yu, p. 1; Portland Rose Festival Association, Photo: Gayle Hoffman, p. 3; John S. Foster, p. 4; © Jeffrey J. Foxx, p. 5; Russell L. Ciochon, p. 6; © Trip/M. Jelliffe, p. 7; © John Elk III, p. 8; Ruthi Soudack, p. 9; Jeff Greenburg, pp. 10, 16; © Trip/B. Gibbs, p. 11; Lyn Hancock, p. 12; © Brian A. Vikander, p. 13; IPS, p. 14; © Trip/S. Grant, p. 15; © Elaine Little/World Photo Images, p. 17; Nancy Smedstad/IPS, p. 18; © Stephen Graham Photography, p. 19; © Trip/M. Ockenden, p. 20; Voscar, The Maine Photographer, p. 21.

First published in this edition in Great Britain by Zero To Ten Limited, part of the Evans Publishing Group, 2A Portman Mansions, Chiltern Street, London W1U 6NR

Reprinted 2006

First published in the United States by Carolrhoda Books, Inc., c/o The Lerner Publishing Group, 241 First Avenue North, Minneapolis, MN 55401 U.S.A.

A CIP catalogue record for this book is available from the British Library.

ISBN 1-84089-323-0
13-digit ISBN (from 1 Jan 2007) 978 1 84089 323 6

Printed in China by WKT Company Limited

Do you celebrate
when you do something great?

You can celebrate winter.

You can celebrate spring.

Celebrate a trip to the park

or a visit from the king.

When something special happens,
get a new hairdo.

Put on your best outfit. Do something
you never thought you'd do!

Get on someone's shoulders
when a parade goes through town.

Or join the marchers
and wave a flag around.

When the day seems special,
bang a drum

or dance a dance.

Run a race.

Is there something
you want to celebrate, too?

Think of time you spend with family

or days you spend with friends.

Celebrate holidays and every day.

Celebrate no matter where,
no matter when!

More about the Pictures

Front cover: In North Korea, children celebrate the fiftieth anniversary of the Workers' Party.

Back cover: This girl is dressed up for the Notting Hill Carnival, which takes place in a West Indian neighbourhood in London.

Page 1: People in Taiwan celebrate with a parade.

Page 3: This girl in Oregon, USA, celebrates winning a rosette in a local parade.

Page 4: Winter snows make kids in Alaska, USA, smile.

Page 5: This boy in Georgia, a country in southeastern Europe, celebrates the coming of spring.

Page 6: It's time for fun at a park in Hanoi, Vietnam.

Page 7: An Ashanti chief visits during a festival in Ghana, a West African country.

Page 8: A girl in Mali, in West Africa, wears a new hairdo for a special day.

Page 9: For the Holi festival in India, people pour bright-coloured powder on their heads and celebrate the end of winter.

Page 10: You have to be tall to see what's going on in Saint Petersburg, Russia.

Page 11: On a London street, English children wave their flag, the Union Jack.

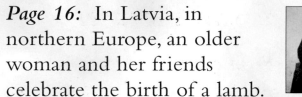

Page 16: In Latvia, in northern Europe, an older woman and her friends celebrate the birth of a lamb.

Page 12: In Nunavut, a territory in northern Canada, a young Inuit child learns to play the drum.

Page 17: Going to school is a good reason to celebrate for these children in Tokyo, Japan.

Page 13: A girl in Laos, a country in Southeast Asia, dances a traditional dance to wish people well.

Page 18: In Minncapolis, in the USA, a grandmother and grandchild celebrate their Ukrainian heritage.

Page 14: In Côte d'Ivoire, a country on the west coast of Africa, a young man takes part in a race.

Page 19: Three friends enjoy just being together in Omaha, Nebraska, USA.

Page 15: To celebrate Thanksgiving, these American children dress up a little differently – as the Statue of Liberty.

Page 20: Celebrating Halloween is popular with these children in London.

Page 21: A young girl celebrates summer in Quebec City, Canada.

A Note to Adults on Sharing This Book

Help your child become a lifelong reader. Read this book together, taking turns as you both read out loud. Look over the photographs and choose your favourites. Sound out new words and come back to them later for review. Then try these "extensions" – activities that extend the experience of reading and build discussion and problem-solving skills.

Talk about Celebrating

All around the world, you can find people celebrating. Discuss with your child the things people celebrate in different countries. What holidays, birthdays and other events do you celebrate? How do your celebrations differ from celebrations in other parts of the world? How are they the same?

Plan Your Next Celebration

With your child, plan your next holiday, birthday or other celebration. Ask your child what decorations will be needed. Make a list of foods you will need. Talk about inviting friends and family. Then work together to complete your plans and make this celebration special.